Introduction to

Real Estate -

Beyond Residential Sales

Real Estate Finance, Property Management, Residential and Commercial Leasing, Investing, 1031 Exchange, Auctions

This book is dedicated to all of you, who want to grow in the exciting field of real estate!

Motivation

This book was written for existing real estate agents as well as those that are considering real estate. It will provide you with an understanding of your different options in the real estate industry, beyond the traditional and very popular residential real estate sales path.

Overview

This book introduces seven areas of real estate every real estate agent should know something about:

Chapter 1 looks at real estate finance.

Chapter 2 looks at property management.

Chapter 3 looks at residential leasing.

Chapter 4 looks at commercial leasing.

Chapter 5 looks at investing in real estate.

Chapter 6 looks at 1031 exchanges.

Chapter 7 looks at real estate auctions.

About the Author

David Gadish, Ph.D., is a tenured university professor, a former management consultant, licensed real estate professional, real estate trainer, and coach.

David is a founding partner at Geffen Real Estate in Beverly Hills, California, where he oversees a team of residential and commercial real estate agents.

David is a professor at the College of Business and Economics, California State University, Los Angeles. He also currently teaches real estate at Touro College Los Angeles, a division of Touro University Worldwide, where he established the current real estate program.

David is also the author of "The Eight Step Strategy for Success in Real Estate Sales: And The 18 Reasons Why Most New Real Estate Agents Fail, Featuring The 13 Key Factors in Selecting a Real Estate Brokerage".

In his spare time, David and his wife and business partner, Orit, raise their four daughters on their over 150 fruit tree orchard in Beverly Hills, California. David Gadish can be reached via text at 310-433-0694 or via email at david@GeffenRealEstate.com.

Legal Disclaimer

Although the author and publisher made every effort to ensure that the information in this book was accurate at press time, the author and publisher do not assume and hereby disclaim any liability to any party for any loss, damage, or disruption caused by errors or omissions.

The author and the publisher disclaim any and all liability to the maximum extent permitted by law if any information, analysis, opinions, advice, and/or recommendations in this book prove to be inaccurate, incomplete, unreliable, or result in any other losses.

The information contained in this book does not constitute legal or financial advice and should never be used without first consulting with legal and other professionals.

The publisher and the author do not make any guarantee or other promise as to any outcomes that may or may not be obtained from using this book's content. You should conduct your own research and due diligence.

Information in this book is based on California specific real estate law and may or may not apply in your state. Laws and regulations referenced in this book are subject to change.

Brief Table of Contents

Table of Contents

Table of Figures

Chapter 1 – Real Estate Finance

Chapter Overview

Chapter 1 looks at what loan officers and mortgage brokers do. It starts by providing a look at the key characteristics of loans. It then proceeds to discuss the four elements of getting a loan.

The chapter then details the financing process and concludes with a discussion of financing options.

By the end of this chapter, you should have an understanding of basic real estate finance and can decide if this is something you want to pursue as a career.

Chapter Outline

Characteristics of Loans

The Four Elements to Getting a Loan

The Financing Process

Financing Options

About Real Estate Finance

Loan officers and mortgage brokers help borrowers with the finance or refinance of their real estate assets. This chapter looks at the basic characteristics of loans, what it takes to get a loan, the financing process, and different types of financing. This will give you an idea if a real estate finance career path is or is not for you.

Loan officers, as well as mortgage brokers, are referred to as lenders in this chapter.

Characteristics of Loans

Interest Rate

Different loans have different interest rates. Generally, the longer the term, the higher the interest rate.

Amortization

Fully amortized loans – Borrower pays principal and interest each month, and by the end of the term, the loan is fully paid off.

Partially amortized loans – Borrower pays principal and interest each month. The amount paid does not result in the loan being fully paid off at the end of the term. There is a final payment to pay the difference called "balloon payment".

Interest Only Loans – Borrower pays interest only for the duration or portion of the loan duration. There is a balloon payment at the end of the term.

Repayment Period

Most often, loans are for 30-year terms. However, there are also loans for 15 and 20-year terms available to borrowers. The longer the term, if all other characteristics are the same, then the smaller are the monthly payments.

Loan to Value (LTV)

Loan to Value (LTV) is a ratio of the loan amount vs. the property's purchase price. For example, an LTV of 90% means that on a $1,000,000 purchase, the buyer pays $100,000 from their funds, and the lender finances the rest ($900,000).

The lower the LTV, the less risky the loan is for lenders. Different loan programs have different maximum LTV requirements.

Mortgage Insurance

Lenders typically require mortgage insurance for loans with higher LTV value and/or borrowers with lower credit scores.

Secondary Financing

Loan to pay part of the down payment for the first loan and/or the closing costs.

Fixed vs. Adjustable-Rate Loans

The interest rate remains the same for fixed-rate loans. For Adjustable-Rate Loans (ARM), the lender can adjust the interest rate, depending on a specific index.

The Four Elements to Getting a Loan

The four elements lenders take into consideration when approving a loan are (see Figure 1):

- Credit (including liabilities and credit history)
- Income
- Assets
- Property to be Acquired

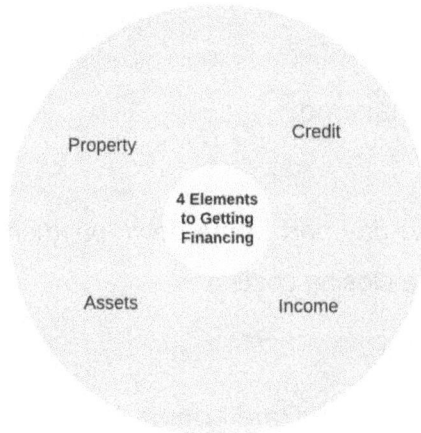

Property

Credit

**4 Elements
to Getting
Financing**

Assets

Income

Figure 1 - Four Elements to Getting Financing

The Financing Process

The financing process consists of possible pre-qualification, pre-approval, conditional commitment, locking the rate and terms, and finally financing the property. The process is outlined in Figure 2.

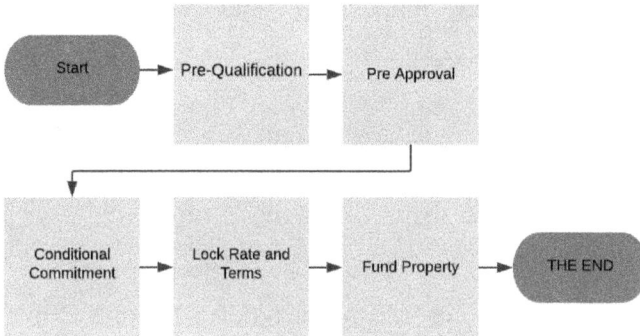

Figure 2 - The Financing Process

Each step in the process is further discussed below.

Pre-Qualification

A buyer approaches a lender to get general information about the loan process and qualification guidelines. This step requires the buyer to verbally provide financial attributes to the lender to determine which loan program is the best fit for a hypothetical purchase price. The potential loan amount and monthly payments are discussed for the buyer to self-determine affordability and sufficient funds with no application or verification completed.

The "pre-qualification" is often used interchangeably with the "pre-approval," so it is highly recommended to get clarification when discussing this with real estate professionals or buyers.

Pre-Approval

This step is more common, making the pre-qualification process obsolete. This process requires the buyer(s) to complete a loan application (usually online or by phone) and authorize the lender to order a credit report to review outstanding liabilities and payment history. The lender then reviews the financial attributes, clarifies employment history and source of down payment and closing costs in the application to ensure accuracy, and then generates an automated disposition in minutes by sending encrypted financial data electronically to Desktop Underwriter or a similar automated underwriting system to approve or decline the application. This process allows the lender to provide the buyer with a pre-approval letter or advance the application to an underwriter for confirmation if the automated system recommends a decline decision.

Conditional Commitment Letter

This is the highest and best step to take, where the lender can provide the buyer with a conditional commitment letter. This is an upgrade to the pre-approval letter. This process requires the borrower to provide the lender with documentation to validate the pre-approval application's financial attributes. This consists of providing the lender the check stubs, W2s, tax returns, and bank, retirement, and investment account statements as needed to comply with loan program guidelines. The lender's underwriter then reviews this documentation to upgrade pre-approval to full approval subject to purchase contract and third-party documentation from vendors providing title and escrow services.

Formal Loan Approval

By the time buyer successfully negotiates the purchase contract, the Conditional Commitment Letter can transition to Loan Approval Letter after escrow and title documentation is reviewed by the underwriter, provided the credit report and income/asset documentation haven't expired. Should any document be about to expire during the escrow period, the buyer should provide the lender with updated documentation making it critical not to get into additional debt and not lose work or get paid less after the loan application is pre-approved. Usually, the loan rate and terms can be locked at this time to ensure the loan approval is stable throughout the escrow period; the Loan Estimate that details the potential closing costs is issued, and the appraisal report is ordered.

Final Loan Approval

Final loan approval occurs after the underwriter reviews the complete file consisting of the fully executed purchase contract package, escrow instructions, preliminary title report, appraisal report, verbal verification of continued employment by a third-party vendor, and updated customer documentation (if necessary) to ensure data is current and in compliance with loan program guidelines. The file is now considered "cleared to close", with the underwriter no longer involved in the closing process.

Funding the Property

The last step in the financing process is getting the loan funded after the file is "cleared to close". However, before the buyer can sign loan documents, the buyer must acknowledge the Closing Disclosure (CD) to confirm the final accounting of closing costs is acceptable. The CD prepared by the lender summarizes the final accounting for all non-recurring and recurring closing costs associated with the home's purchase. The accounting is a collaboration between the lender and escrow, providing detail on the actual costs to close. Federal laws require the CD to be acknowledged by the buyer at least three days before signing loan documents, so this step is crucial for closing on time.

If the accounting is in error for any reason, releasing a new CD can delay closing until the new three-day time period has passed. Assuming the final accounting is within legal parameters from what was on the Loan Estimate when the purchase contract was provided, the buyer signs the loan documents after three days pass. Then later, the same day or next, the escrow company faxes/emails copy of signed loan documents to the lender with the proof they received the balance of funds needed to close the transaction from the buyer, and the lender funds the loan the same day.

Financing Options

A variety of financing options are available for a buyer interested in submitting an offer for a property. The following sections describe these types of financing, as well as others that are available for buyers (see Figure 3).

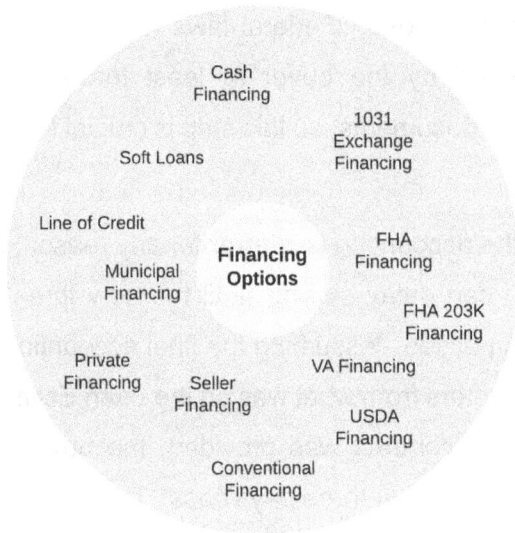

Cash Financing

1031 Exchange Financing

Soft Loans

Line of Credit

Financing Options

FHA Financing

Municipal Financing

FHA 203K Financing

Private Financing

VA Financing

Seller Financing

USDA Financing

Conventional Financing

Figure 3 - Types of Real Estate Financing

Conventional Financing

Conventional loans are perhaps the most common type of financing used by buyers. Conventional loans usually require 20% down, an appraisal substantiating the loan to value ratio, and specific habitability requirements related to the property's condition. Still, relative to an FHA loan, these conditions are usually few and liberal.

If the down payment is (typically) less than 20%, mortgage insurance may be required and could increase the monthly payment.

Individual lenders may have additional property requirements that other lenders may not have. For example, some lenders may require Section 1 Termite clearance while others do not. Conventional loans typically take up to 30 days to fund.

Cash, Hard Money, and Line of Credit Financing

When a buyer specifies that they are offering "Cash", the listing agent must review the buyer's proof of funds to ensure that funds are sufficient, liquid, and dated within the past 30 days. Cash offers are usually the most appealing to sellers because funds are immediately available, and the offer does not carry a loan contingency. For cash offers, liquid funds can be transferred to the closing company within a day if desired.

Examples of liquid funds include funds held in a bank and investments like stocks and Certificate of Deposits (CDs). For investments, you must consider potential penalties and value losses if the buyer withdraws funds. If a fee is assessed for withdrawing funds, you must ensure that funds are still sufficient for purchase.

If a buyer is obtaining a "Hard Money Loan" or a "Line of Credit" aka "HELOC," and their offer is one of the strongest, you should contact the lender and buyer. Identify the type of documentation that has been reviewed by the lender, what the loan is contingent upon, is the line of credit based on home equity that the lender may withdraw, etc.?

Although buyers' agents designate them as "cash", these offers are not cash. Listing agents should also inquire how much of a down payment the buyer is offering and request proof of funds for that down payment.

FHA Financing

FHA loans are mortgages insured and backed by the Federal Housing Administration (FHA) and are issued by FHA approved lenders. These loans require a lower down payment and lower credit scores than conventional loans. Their qualifying guidelines are designed to accommodate low and moderate-income borrowers. They usually require as little as 3.5% down. This type of loan is prevalent among first-time homebuyers and typically takes 45 days to fund. These loans typically require paying for mortgage insurance as well as part of the loan.

FHA loans require that an appraiser inspect the property to appraise it and identify any health and safety issues.

FHA buyer qualifications change from time to time, as governments may wish to make homes more or less accessible to buyers at different times. For example, in the past, FHA loans required Section 1 Termite Repairs to be completed and an operable stove to be installed before the close of escrow.

Note: FHA offers on properties with an HOA (Homeowners Association) cannot be considered unless the HOA is FHA approved. It is imperative to determine if an HOA is FHA approved as early as possible in the process. Sometimes the HOA's records may be outdated and will not indicate FHA approval.

If an HOA does not indicate FHA approval, check the US Department of Housing and Urban Development (HUD) website to see if the complex is FHA approved. It is the absolute authority on this matter. Housing and Urban Development (HUD) website: https://entp.hud.gov/idapp/html/condlook.cfm

FHA 203K Financing

An FHA 203K loan is a renovation mortgage sponsored by the Federal Housing Administration (FHA).

An FHA 203K loan enables buyers to finance a home's purchase and the cost to rehabilitate it. A portion of the loan is used to pay the seller for the purchase, and the remaining funds are placed in an escrow account and released to the vendor(s) as renovations/repairs are completed.

The appraisal process for an FHA 203K loan is relatively long as all repairs must first be assessed. Costs for each repair or renovation must be estimated, and then buyer must qualify for the mortgage to cover these costs. The buyer selects a 203(k) consultant and a general contractor to work with and submits documentation listing repairs to be made, which is provided to the appraiser to provide an "as-repaired appraisal", which is an estimate of the fair market value after the property has been repaired.

There is no need to wait for the repairs to be completed before the lender will fund the transaction. The lengthy appraisal process means these loans typically take 45-60 days to close.

VA Financing

This type of financing is guaranteed by the United States Department of Veterans Affairs (VA) for qualified veterans of military service. VA loans typically require no down payment (0% down) and include lender terms and conditions comparable to an FHA loan. VA loans usually take 30-60 days to fund.

USDA Financing

This type of financing is guaranteed by the United States Department of Agriculture (USDA) for individuals purchasing homes in rural and certain pockets of suburban areas. The USDA guarantees mortgages issued by participating lenders. The USDA also issues loans directly to low and very-low-income applicants. They are low-interest mortgages with zero down payment.

The purpose of these loans is to promote ownership in defined rural areas of the country to drive community development in agricultural areas. Income qualification for this type of loan is capped at 150% of the median income for that area.

Many lenders are reluctant to offer loans for these markets because they present a high-risk to the lender. Properties in these markets may quickly lose significant value due to severe weather, unstable dependence on local companies, and other events that can devastate local economies.

The USDA's home financing program is designed to compensate for this market gap/risk aversion. These loans include lender terms and conditions comparable to an FHA loan. USDA loans usually take 30-60 days to fund.

1031 Exchange Financing

The buyer obtains funding for this type of financing by selling a property that they previously owned. Funds from the sale are usually held by a qualified intermediary and can be used to purchase a different property.

1031 exchange is defined under section 1031 of the IRS Code. A 1031 exchange allows an investor to defer paying capital gains taxes on an Investment property when it is sold, as long as another like-kind property is purchased with the funds from the first property's sale.

1031 exchange is discussed in more detail in a later chapter.

Seller Financing

In seller financing, the seller assumes the role of a lender. The seller extends credit to the buyer for the purchase, less the down payment. Buyer and seller sign a promissory note. They record a mortgage or deed of trust with the public recorder's office. The majority of these loans are short-term, with a balloon payment due in, say, five years.

The idea is that within a few years, the home will have gained enough in value, or the buyers' financial situation would have improved so that the buyer can refinance with a traditional lender.

Private Financing

Private lenders are not affiliated with a bank or other financial institution. Private lenders use their capital to finance real estate purchases and work directly with the borrower. Investors or banks or both generally fund them. They provide short-term loans to investors for the purchase or renovation of investment properties.

Private loans are usually processed much faster than other types of loans and have more lenient buyer qualification criteria, may not have appraisal contingencies, and are generally only offered to well-established investor buyers.

Many buyer's agents refer to these loans as cash on their offers, but they are not cash. This type of financing still has qualifying criteria, and most of the time, requires a down payment from the buyer.

Private lenders are still subject to state and federal law but are significantly less regulated and can be more flexible in the types of loans they can make and who they choose to lend to.

Line of Credit

Buyers may wish to finance their offer with a line of credit. The most common line of credit is the Home Equity Line of Credit (HELOC). HELOC loans are based on the difference between your current home's value and your current mortgage balance.

Buyers' agents often present lines of credit as cash, but they are not cash. The possibility that a line of credit may be revoked due to depreciating property values or other reasons also means that a line of credit is not a dependable source of funds.

Other lines of credit include lines extended to investors by capital groups. While these capital groups do have the cash to pay, and the line of credit is more or less assured, these financing types often carry "subject to appraisal" or "back-end buyer needed" conditions.

Still, most lines of credit rank higher than conventional or FHA loans in sellers' eyes because a line of credit funds faster and carries fewer conditions than a conventional or FHA loan.

Soft Loans

Soft loans are usually provided by government entities or nonprofit organizations and often do not require the buyer to repay the loan until the buyer resells the property. Some entities require that low levels of interest accrue over this period (usually, these rates are comparable with inflation figures), while others charge no interest at all.

Municipal Financing

Typically, municipal loans are designated for Neighborhood Stabilization Programs (NSP). These are designed to draw homeowners into areas with a high volume of rented properties and communities municipal governments would like to see improved. It is assumed that homeowners will have a greater vested interest in improving these communities than the tenants of rented properties.

There are usually caps on municipal loans, required concessions, and limitations on which properties can qualify. For example, some municipal loans may only be offered on foreclosed homes.

Municipal loans for Neighborhood Stabilization (NSP) programs are usually a type of soft loan that gives homeowners an incentive to choose a property in less desirable neighborhoods. The caps on these loans typically mean they are used more like a second loan in addition to a buyer's first loan.

Other municipal loans are city or county backed loans. These loans are usually designated only for specific properties, specific blocks, or particular buildings that the city or county wishes to develop or restore.

Chapter 2 - Property Management

Chapter Overview

Chapter 2 provides a look at what property managers do. It starts by signing a management contract and then defining and deploying takeover procedures.

It looks at the ongoing reporting relationship with the owners, establishing rents, marketing properties for lease, screening tenants, negotiating leases, helping tenants move in, collecting rents, renewing leases, handling tenant issues as they arise, and assisting tenants with moveouts

The chapter concludes with a discussion about handling legal matters, performing regular inspections, handling maintenance, repairs, and remodeling, and of course, handling financial matters and reporting those to the owners.

By the end of this chapter, you should have a basic understanding of property management and can decide if this is something you want to pursue as a career.

Chapter Outline

Define and Sign a Management Contract

Define and Deploy Takeover Procedures

Ongoing Relationship with Owner/Representative

Evaluate the Property to Establish Rents

Market the Property for Lease

Tenant Screening, Selection, and Lease Negotiations

Tenant Move-In

Rent Collection

Lease Renewals

Tenant Relations

Tenant Move Out

Tenancy Termination

Legal

Inspections

Financial Reporting

Maintenance, Repair, Remodeling

About Property Management

Many owners of commercial assets choose to hire professional property managers or management companies to manage their real estate assets. Consider property management as a system that involves many components that work together to achieve a common goal. It takes a detail-oriented person to see and be able to oversee the big picture.

Knowing property management can help you manage your properties as well one day.

This chapter provides an overview of the various activities property managers handle (See Figure 4 below).

Define / Sign
Management
Contract

Define / Deploy
Takeover
Procedure

Maintenance /
Repair /
Remodeling

Establish Rents

Financial
Reporting

**Property
Management**

Market Property
for Lease

Inspections

Tenant
Relations

Tenant
Screening /
Selection

Tenant Move
Out

Tenant Move In

Lease
Negotiations

Tenant
Termination /
Legal

Rent Collection

Lease Renewals

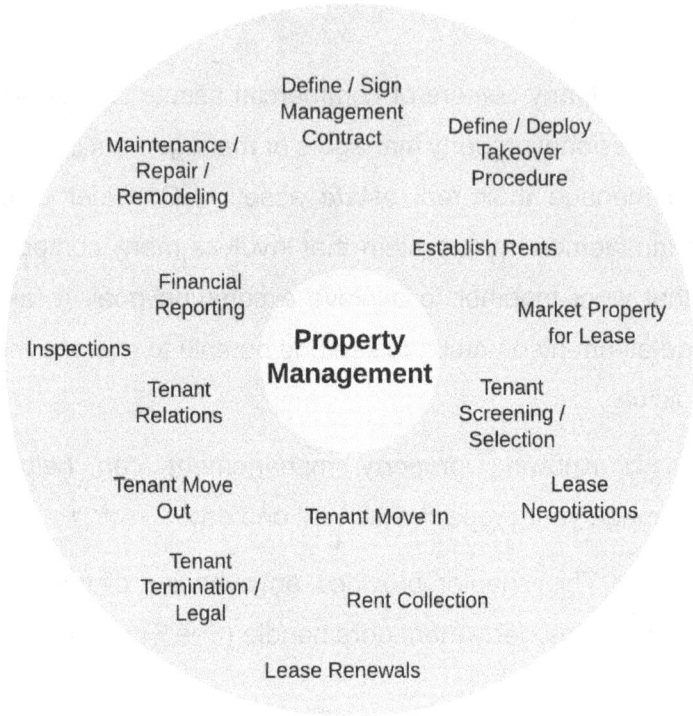

Figure 4 - Key Property Management Activities

Key property management activities are discussed in the following sections.

Define and Sign a Management Contract

You should work with your client to define and sign an agreement to manage and lease real estate. A real estate management contract typically includes:

- The parties to the contract
- The duration of the contract
- Authority and responsibilities of the management company (you)
- Responsibilities of the owner
- Exclusions
- Termination
- Fees
- Signatures

Define and Deploy Takeover Procedures

Once the management contract is signed, it is time to transfer responsibilities. You should request all data necessary for the efficient operation of the property.

Ongoing Relationship with Owner/Representative

You should provide your client with monthly reports, including financial reports. You should keep an open communication channel with them, informing them of any issues that require their attention as they arise.

Evaluate the Property to Establish Rents

You should conduct a property and market analysis, provide you with lease values of comparable properties in the vicinity of the subject property and make a recommendation of likely lease price(s).

Market the Property for Lease

You should prepare the property for lease, which may include cleanup and/or remodeling. The next steps include marketing the property using traditional and online marketing strategies, handling showings to prospective tenants, and providing and collecting applications.

Tenant Screening, Selection, and Lease Negotiations

You should provide each prospective tenant with a lease application and run credit and background checks if they consent to it.   There are several excellent online applications on the market that can help you with tenant screening.   The prospective tenant typically pays for the service.   Chapter 17 provides additional details on tenant screening and lease negotiations.

Tenant Move-In

Once you have identified a qualified tenant, you should complete a leasing agreement, confirm the move-in date with the tenant, review lease guidelines with the tenant, and ensure all agreements have been properly executed.

You should use the C.A.R Residential Lease/Month-to-Month Rental Agreement (LR) form for residential leases. For commercial leases, you should use the C.A.R. Commercial Lease Agreement (CL) or the AIR CRE Contracts, based on the property type.

Once there is a fully executed lease, you should collect the first month's rent and the security deposit and conduct a walkthrough of the property with the tenant(s). You should use the C.A.R. MIMO form to document the move-in condition of each item listed on the form, either as new, satisfactory/clean, or other, and comments should be noted to explain the condition. Photos should be taken as well during the move-in walkthrough to document the condition of the property. The tenant(s) should review, initial, and sign the form, and you should provide it to the owner for review, initials, and signature as well.

Rent Collection

You or the owner will be collecting rents, pursuing late payments, issuing notices to pay rent or quit, and enforcing late fees.

Typically you or the owner should maintain three trust accounts (for properties with a large number of tenants):

- Operating account
- Reserve fund account
- Security deposit account

Lease Renewals

Steady tenants with a good payment history are assets. The quality of your tenants and existing market conditions will dictate the parameters of a lease extension. To extend the term of an existing lease, you can use the

C.A.R. Extension of Lease (EL) form. Any new or modified terms can be specified on this form.

Tenant Relations

You should maintain a good relationship with the tenant(s). You might check in with them periodically to see how things are going. You should be responsive within reason to their requests.

Tenant Move Out

Once the tenant(s) are ready to move out, you should conduct a move out walkthrough with the tenant(s) and use and document findings in the C.A.R. MIMO form. Look for changes in property condition at move-in, and take photos to document each change. The "move out" column should be completed, specifying the condition of each item listed as either satisfactory or requiring a deposit deduction, and comments should be noted. The tenant will review, initial, and sign the "Move Out" section of the form, and it should be provided to the owner for initial and signature as well. Provide the tenant with a copy of the fully executed MIMO form and calculate any withholdings. Before returning the security deposit, subtract the cost of repairs and explain to the tenant(s) what will be withheld from their deposit and why. The unit should have sales cleaning performed, and any necessary repairs made, and the property should be rekeyed. You should market the property to identify the next qualified tenant.

Tenancy Termination

A lease may expire, and the tenant may not wish to extend the lease. In the event a quality tenant wishes to leave the property, you should try to understand why this is happening and see if they can reverse the decision by asking what the reason is for termination.

If the tenant insists on moving on, the security deposit should be returned, less the portion kept for damages.

A tenant may abandon the property, a tenant may surrender the property by mutual agreement, or the tenant may be evicted.

Legal

You should understand and abide by the latest local, state, and federal laws that apply to leasing and maintaining rental properties. You should consult with a qualified attorney if and when necessary.

Inspections

You should perform periodic inspections looking for health and safety hazards, code violations, lease violations, and other things that may require repairs. You should send the owner periodic reports on the condition of the property.

Financial Reporting

You (if applicable) should provide accounting property management services and make payments on the owner's behalf. Ongoing monthly, quarterly, and annual reporting should be provided.

Maintenance, Repair, Remodeling

You should have a network of licensed, bonded, and fully insured vendors who have been vetted for good quality work and reasonable pricing. You should assign jobs to different parties based on who will do the best job for the best price. You should maintain and monitor a 24-hour emergency repair hotline. You could also oversee more extensive renovation or rehab projects.

Specialized property management companies tend to create plans that include:

- Ongoing maintenance
- Preventative maintenance
- Handling maintenance requests
- Routine inspections

Chapter 3 - Residential Leasing

Chapter Overview

Chapter 17 looks at some of what residential agents do. It introduces the steps involved in the residential leasing process. It looks at the possible terms of the lease and commission. It proceeds to discuss property marketing and showings.

The chapter proceeds to discuss tenant screening, the lease application, as well as lease negotiations. The chapter concludes by discussing the three essential topics of contract management, start of lease term activities, and applicable federal and state laws.

By the end of this chapter, you should have an understanding of residential leasing and can decide if this is something you want to pursue as a career.

Chapter Outline

Defining the Terms of the Lease

Commission to Agent(s)

Marketing a Property for Lease

Showing the Property

Tenant Screening

The Lease Application

Reading a Typical Lease Application

Identifying Red Flags on Lease Applications

Common Problems with Lease Applications

Lease Application Denial Letter

Lease Terms

Lease Negotiations

Lease Contract Management

Start of Lease Term

Federal and State Laws

About Residential Leasing

Leasing a residential property (condos, apartments, or single-family homes) includes the following seven steps. You and the landlord should first define the lease terms, then market the property for lease, show the property to prospective tenants, screen the tenants, negotiate the lease, and finally, manage the lease terms. These steps are discussed in detail in the following sections.

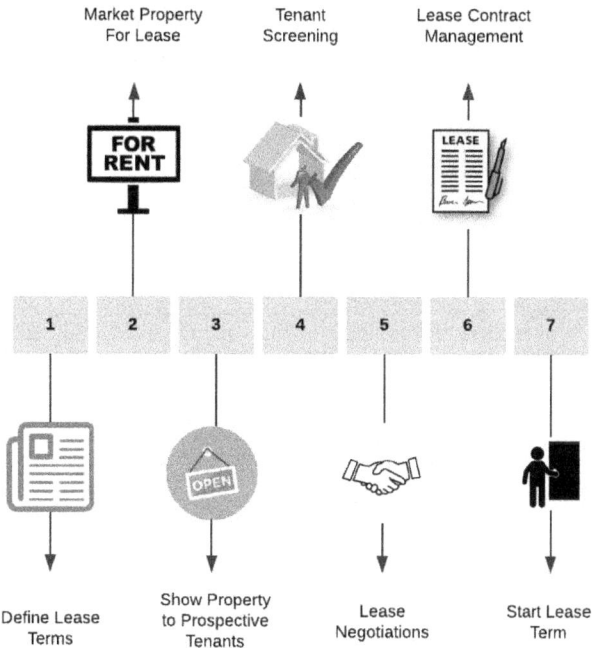

Market Property For Lease	Tenant Screening	Lease Contract Management

| 1 | 2 | 3 | 4 | 5 | 6 | 7 |

| Define Lease Terms | Show Property to Prospective Tenants | Lease Negotiations | Start Lease Term |

Figure 5 - The Residential Leasing Process

Defining the Terms of the Lease

You should provide the landlord with a valuation. The valuation should include comparables. Ideally, you should provide the owner with details of each property leased within the past three months within a quarter of a mile of the subject property. If there are insufficient comparables, you should expand the search for comparables to 6 months and/or 0.5 miles.

Work with the landlord to define the following lease terms:

- Monthly Rent Amount (based on the comparables)
- Deposit Amount
- Is water included or excluded?
- Is gas included, excluded, or not applicable?
- Is electricity included or excluded?
- Is yard maintenance service included or excluded?
- Are pets allowed? Cats? Dogs? Small only? Any size?
- If there is an HOA, does the tenant pay the HOA fee? What is included?

Commission to Agent(s)

You should define the commission payable to you. Typically in Los Angeles County, the commission can be either 5% or 6% for residential transactions. The commission should be split between the agent representing the buyer and the agent representing the seller. It is also reasonable to offer a minimum commission if this is a low valued/short term lease.

Marketing a Property for Lease

You will market the property for lease based on the above-proposed terms of a lease. Your marketing efforts should aim at a minimum to include:

- Photos and videos created by a professional photographer.
- A virtual 3D tour
- Placing the property on the local MLS
- Advertising the property on Apartments.com
- Placing a For Lease sign (if permitted)
- Advertising the property on Craigslist.com
- Advertising the property on Social Media

For luxury properties, a dedicated website to market the property is suggested.

Showing the Property

You should conduct open houses (or virtual open houses). The open houses should be marketed on the MLS as well as social media.

You should also allow for private showings upon request.

Tenant Screening

Screening candidate tenants is one of the essential parts of the leasing process. It helps evaluate the risk and helps choose the best quality tenants from the various applicants. Ensuring good quality tenants can mean increased revenue. It also enhances the reputation of a property. Good tenants stay longer, reduce periods of vacancy, which increases revenues, and reduces stress for property owners and managers.

Every applicant must be treated equally in the screening process. Always follow established procedures and ask for identification first.

Ideally, you want a tenant with a stable job, good credit history, and no criminal record. You want the tenant to afford the rent and want them to stay at the property for the duration you have it available for lease.

You should use a reputable online screening service that will run each prospect's credit report and background check and allow the prospects to upload all relevant documents for your review.

A prospective tenant that is not willing to register and pay for such services is not serious. This allows you to eliminate some candidates.

Once the landlord reviews the tenant's package you provided them, they can request additional documentation if the package is not complete or reject the prospective tenant based on the partial package.

Once the package is complete, you should conduct a comprehensive review of the package and interview the candidate.

You should report the outcome of the interview with the landlord and make a recommendation. You can then ask the landlord if they wish to proceed to meet the candidate tenant at the property before moving to the contract stage or if they wish to pass.

The Lease Application

The lease application presents a tenant's rental history. Proper handling of a lease application is needed to protect your business, yourself, and your reputation.

You should use a lease application from a reputable source, know what information to collect, learn how to interpret the information you collect, know how to verify the information, look out for red flags, understand the laws related to residential leasing, and avoid actions that may be discriminatory.

Reading a Typical Lease Application

You need to know how to read, understand, and use the lease application to achieve your leasing goals.

Many agents, landlords, and property managers take the easy way out by just glancing at the income listed and then running a credit report. Finding the right tenant requires a thorough analysis.

A typical lease application includes personal information, property details, residence history, employment, income information, financial information, and information about pets and vehicles (see Figure 6). These are discussed in the following sections.

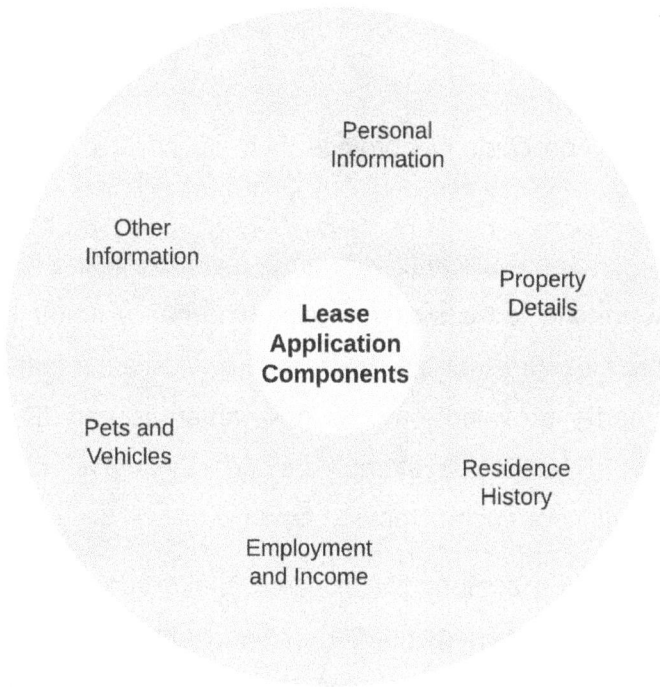

Personal
Information

Other
Information

Property
Details

**Lease
Application
Components**

Pets and
Vehicles

Residence
History

Employment
and Income

Figure 6 - Lease Application Components

Personal Information

Personal information is needed to verify the identity of the individuals applying to lease the property and getting an idea of who is applying. You or the landlord should gather some essential information to keep on file if you want to contact the applicant or file an unlawful detainer down the road.

Name - Applicants will provide their first, middle, and last names.

Some applicants with an unfavorable lease history may pretend to be someone else who has a better track record. Ensure that the name on the application matches the name provided on any government-issued ID you collect. Online systems provide automatic identity verification for each screening report.

When screening applicants, make sure the name provided is their legal name. Also, maintaining correct names for all tenants can help you keep tenants accountable if there are any issues later on that require an eviction or collections.

Social Security Number - It is possible to collect this on a standard lease application. However, some suggest you do not require a social security number on a lease application. Many agents and property managers require an SSN or even reject applicants who do not provide one. Doing this may be interpreted as discriminating against applicants based on their national origin, a federally protected class. Such action can result in a substantial fine.

You do not need an SSN to run tenant screening reports! Online tenant screening systems provide full tenant screening reports that do not require the applicant's SSN.

If you feel that you must have an SSN to keep on file for tenants, you should consider asking for the SSN during the lease signing process and not during the lease application process.

Other occupants - Applicants should always list the other individuals who will occupy the unit. It is essential to know exactly who will be living there. Make sure you are collecting complete information from all adult occupants. With that information, you can determine if the applicant(s) will be a good fit for the property,

Let us look at two scenarios:

A couple applies. They specify that the other occupants are their ten children and four parents. You can factor this into your decision-making process and determine if your property's size can accommodate the total number of occupants.

An individual applies. In the "Other Occupants" section, another individual is listed who is over 18 years of age. You should make sure that the other occupant applies and is screened separately as well.

Phone Numbers – Beneficial to have in case you need to ask any follow-up questions during your screening process. You can use them to get in touch with tenants if you need to down the road, for example, to track down those who have not paid rent.

Date of Birth - Helps you verify the candidate's identity. Make sure that the date of birth matches with any identification provided by an applicant. Some screening reports may also provide the date of birth for the applicant, in which case you can double-check the information to make sure everything matches. The date of birth also lets you determine whether or not an occupant needs to complete an application. For example, you can not hold minors responsible for rent, so you would not screen them.

Age is a protected class, so you cannot use age as a basis for legally denying an applicant. Developing and applying screening criteria equally to all applicants helps protect you if you ask for the date of birth on your lease application.

Government-Issued Identification - Most lease applications request the applicant to include information related to government-issued identification (ID type, ID number, issuing government agency, and expiration date). You should make sure that all of the information matches to ensure there is no misrepresentation.

Property Details

Information about the property you are leasing should be included on a lease application to ensure you are on the same page with the applicant(s). It also helps you keep applications organized in case you are working with multiple vacancies simultaneously.

The property address, rent amount, and the security deposit should be included. This reminds the applicant(s) what you are asking for and saves everyone's time if the amounts exceed the applicant's budget.

Residence History

Reviewing an applicant's residence history is essential to the decision you will make about each applicant. It includes the following:

Current Residence - An applicant's current residence is the first step, looking back at the residence history.

Residence Type - The applicant can indicate whether they are currently living in a leased unit or in a property they own. If an applicant currently lives in a leased unit, you can contact the current landlord and confirm move-in/move-out dates. For applicants who live in a property they own, find out why they want to move into the leased property.

Current address – Using the current address, you can verify that you are speaking with the actual landlord. Screening reports usually have the address history, so you can check to see that the lease application's address matches the landlord reference check and the address history on the screening reports. By comparing, you can identify red flags on a lease application.

Move-in / move-out dates – Used for cross-referencing when contacting the landlord. A large, unexplained gap in residence can indicate that the applicant is trying to hide a negative lease experience with a previous landlord. You should make sure an applicant's residence history is reported.

Landlord name and contact information – It is crucial to contact landlord references to learn more about the applicant and verify lease history. Missing the landlord's name and contact information is a big red flag.

An applicant may list a friend or relative instead of the actual landlord. One thing you can do when you call the landlord is not to provide the landlord with any of the information you are asking about. Let the landlord provide you the detail about the property address, rent amount, and move-in dates. An actual landlord will be able to provide you with this information, so you can quickly tell if something unethical is happening.

Reason for moving out – Reasonable responses include relocating for work or looking for a larger place. Leaving this field blank is a red flag. Moving out due to eviction is another red flag.

Check the reason for moving out when you contact references. For example, if the applicant lists they are moving for a new job, you should be able to contact the current and previous employers to verify this information.

Previous Residence(s) -   It is critical to contact previous landlords. The current landlord might not tell the whole truth about a bad tenant because they may just want to get rid of the tenant. Previous landlords have no reason to hide such information.

Employment and Income Information

You want to know if the applicant makes enough monthly income to cover the rent and other living expenses. You also want to make sure that the source of income is reasonably stable.

Employer information includes the employer name, address, supervisor/HR manager name. Use this information to perform an employment verification. You should gather proof of income from the applicant (pay stubs, W-2s) and ensure that the employer information matches up. When you contact the employer, have them verify all the information provided by the applicant. Any inconsistencies between the employer and the lease application should be investigated.

By law, you cannot discriminate against the type of income, so it's essential to account for the various types of income provided.

When defining your tenant screening criteria, specify a minimum rent to income ratio you are comfortable with (a typical rent to income ratio is 30%).

Pets and Vehicles

Help make sure there is a good fit between the applicant and your policies. For instance, if you only have one available parking space for the property you are renting, and you see two vehicles listed on the lease application, you may want to contact the applicant to discuss this before moving further with the application.

This section of the lease application serves as a reference later. For example, if an applicant indicates one dog on their application, but you later find out that the tenant has six dogs, you will have the lease application to reference for any action you might need to take.

Some applicants may have a service animal or an emotional support animal. It may appear discriminatory to reject applicants because they have such an animal, even with a no-pets policy in place.

Most lease applications have a miscellaneous section, which may include questions about evictions, bankruptcies, and felony convictions.

These questions can also help pre-screen applicants before you move forward. You can usually verify the answers provided by running tenant screening reports on the applicant.

Identifying Red Flags on Lease Applications

Aside from the obvious indicators such as low credit score and insufficient income, there are other details on a lease application that may point to an unqualified tenant. Identifying these will help you minimize problems down the road.

Encountering any of the following red flags requires additional research for disqualification:

- Contact information not provided for current/previous landlord
- Credit report provided by the applicant – and applicant is not willing to have you run a report

- Currently unemployed and/or no income
- Frequent changes of residence
- Income is unverifiable
- Incomplete information provided
- Information provided does not match screening reports
- The applicant is breaking the lease with their current landlord
- The applicant is in a rush

Common Problems with Lease Applications

The tenant application form you use is the basis of your tenant screening process. With a thorough lease application, you reduce your legal risk and maximize your chances of finding a good tenant.

More and more brokerages use online screening services. These services allow the applicants to apply online (they pay for the service). The applicants upload documents, and the service runs all the checks. You then review all materials and request any information and/or documents that may be missing. Next, you proceed to discuss the applicants' qualifications with the owner.

Lease Application Denial Letter

Denying applicants is unavoidable when handling properties for lease.

It is crucial to ensure you treat applicants fairly and not engage in any discriminatory practices when denying an applicant. Common reasons to deny lease applicants:

- Co-applicant/guarantor was denied
- Credit score or credit report
- Income-to-rent ratio
- Incomplete lease application or misrepresentation on the application
- Unfavorable residence history
- Unverifiable income

You need to make sure you are applying the same denial criteria equally to all applicants. It is best to record your acceptance/rejection ranges for each factor you will be evaluating.

Evaluate applicants in the order in which you receive their information. When you receive a completed application package from an applicant, you should document the time you received it and apply your rejection policy before moving on to the next person who applies. You would ideally accept the first applicant that meets your minimum criteria and stop looking at additional applicants.

Letting applicants know when they are rejected is a critical step required to minimize legal issues. According to the Fair Credit Reporting Act (FCRA), you must provide a lease application denial letter if you reject an applicant based in whole or in part on any consumer reports. That is, if a credit report, credit score, background, or eviction report is factored into your rejection decision, then you must notify the applicant.

Lease Terms

A typical residential lease includes the following terms/clauses (see Figure 7):

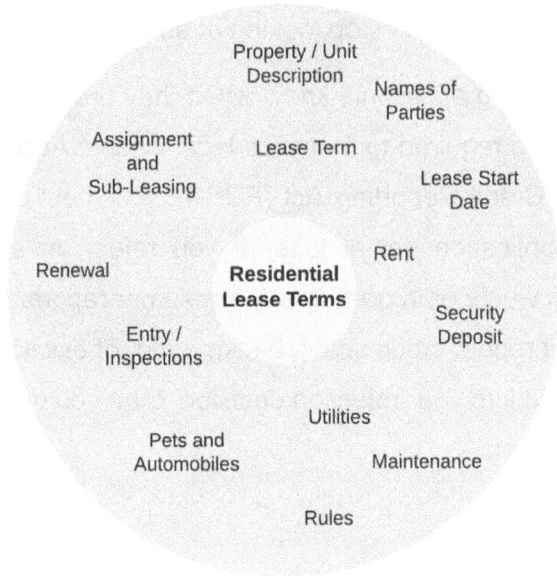

Figure 7 - Typical Residential Lease Terms

- **Property / Unit description** – address and property condition (attach a walkthrough form)
- **Names of parties** - landlord / tenant(s), and possibly co-signers (e.g. parents of university students)
- **Lease term** – Typically one year term
- **Lease start date**
- **Rent** – amount and due dates
- **Security deposit** – in the event of damages to the unit

- **Utilities** – which party pays for what
- **Maintenance** – which party pays for what
- **Rules** – of the building, HOA, governing the tenant's use of the unit and common areas
- **Pets and Automobiles** – types of pets, number of pets, number of automobile parking spots, guest parking
- **Entry / Inspections** – emergency entry, notice ahead of an inspection
- **Renewal** – Notice to be provided before the renewal date, including changes to rent
- **Assignment and Sub-Leasing**
- **Defects** – disclose any known defects

Lease Negotiations

The prospective tenant may agree to all of your proposed terms for the lease, or they may not. The prospective tenant should be aware of the lease terms advertised but may counter with their terms. You should shield the owner from direct contact by the tenant at this stage.

Terms that may be negotiated include:

- Monthly rent amount

- Deposit amount
- Move-in date
- Term of lease
- Who pays for utilities and services

You should provide the property owner with the terms requested and make a recommendation to accept or suggestions on how to counter each term. You should also explain to the property owner your reasoning for the proposed response.

Once the property owner approves the counter terms, you will take them to the prospective tenant. The process may iterate several times until reaching an agreement or realizing an agreement can not be reached.

Lease Contract Management

You can use the Residential Lease or Month-to-Month Lease Agreement (C.A.R. Form LR). You should use an electronic signature service such as DocuSign.com to have the property owner and the tenant(s) sign the lease.

Start of Lease Term

The tenant can either mail you the first month's rent plus deposit or meet you or the landlord at the property and provided it to you at the time of the final walkthrough. Once the walkthrough has been completed, and the tenant has provided payment, keys to the property should be provided to the tenant. You should receive the commission payment and, in turn, issue a check to the tenant's agent if there was one.

Federal and State Laws

You should be aware of several federal and state laws and operate, having them in mind. They include:

- Antitrust Laws
- Megan's Law
- Lead-Based Paint Hazard Reduction Act
- Fair Housing Act
- Americans with Disabilities Act (ADA)
- Equal Credit Opportunity Act (ECOA)
- Fair Credit Reporting Act (FCRA)
- Servicemembers Civil Relief Act (SCRA)

Chapter 4 - Commercial Leasing

Chapter Overview

Chapter 18 looks at some of what commercial leasing agents do. It starts with reviewing the components of a commercial leasing application package and then looks at such applications' review process.

The chapter proceeds to survey the different types of commercial leases and the key terms included in them.

By the end of this chapter, you should have a basic understanding of commercial leasing and can decide if this is something you want to pursue as a career.

Chapter Outline

Components of a Commercial Leasing Application Package

Application Review

Types of Commercial Leases

Typical Terms of Commercial Leases

About Commercial Leasing

Commercial tenant applications are more complex than residential ones. They require information about the business and the individual(s) overseeing the business and/or looking to lease on its behalf.

Components of a Commercial Leasing Application Package

Commercial applications typically require:

- Description of the business / how it operates
- Lease signer's name, role in the business (Owner, CEO, etc.)
- Owners'/Management names, contact information, and biographies
- Financials of the business
- Planned improvements (if any) to the space being leased
- Commercial lease history: names and contact information of past landlords

A typical package includes the application as well as a combination of some or all of the following documents:

- Business Plan
- Franchise Agreement
- Organizing documents (Articles of Incorporation, LLC Agreement, etc.)
- Personal financial statement
- Budget
- Profit and Loss Statement
- Resumes of key individuals
- Tax returns (corporate and / or personal)
- IDs of the individuals that will sign the lease

Application Review

Small and medium-sized business owners are often required to guarantee the lease personally. Screening of the individuals signing the lease, business owners, and/or top management may be necessary once you determine that the business may be a fit for the property you are leasing. You should speak with the applicant(s), owners and/or management, as well as past landlords.

You should review financials to make sure they indicate a stable or growing business, with a realistic multi-year business plan and budget. You should also make sure the management has the experience to run this business.

For situations where the business and its financials are more complex, you or the landlord might want to have a CPA and/or attorney review the application package as well.

Once a prospective tenant's application package has been reviewed and appears to be a fit, lease negotiations should commence. Lease negotiations involve the review and countering of different lease terms. Types of commercial leases, as well as possible lease terms, are presented next.

Types of Commercial Leases

There are five primary types of commercial leases:

- **Straight Lease/Gross Lease** – tenant pays a fixed amount, and the landlord pays all other expenses.
- **Net Lease** – Tenant pays utilities, taxes, and special assessments in addition to the rent.
- **Net-Net Lease** – Same as a Net lease, but tenant also pays insurance premiums.
- **Triple Net Lease** – Same as Net-Net lease, but tenant also pays for repairs and maintenance.
- **Percentage Lease** – tenant pays fixed lease amount and a percentage of gross income in

excess of a minimum amount. This type of lease is commonly used for retail properties.

Typical Terms of Commercial Leases

Typical lease terms/clauses in commercial leases include the following:

- **Legal description** - of the location offered for lease.
- **Existing/proposed floor plans** – of the location.
- **Square footage (SF)**
  - Usable SF – Actual space tenant is to occupy exclusively, without considering the common areas.
  - Rentable SF – Usable SF plus a portion of the building's common areas, such as hallways, lobbies, and storage rooms (inside measurements)
  - Gross SF – The building's entire floor area is measured from the outside.
- **R/U Ratio** – the Rentable SF divided by the Usable SF. The larger this number is, the more the tenant pays towards maintaining common

areas (if the price per SF is the same when comparing buildings).

- **Date of possession** – Date when the tenant is provided with the keys and gains access to the property. If there is a period of time for renovations, the possession date is prior to the lease start date.

- **Lease start date** – Date when the tenant can move. If there is a significant build-out or remodel, the lease start date may be uncertain and therefore specified as "X days after build-out (or remodel) is complete."

- **Tenant Improvement Allowance (TIA)** – Amount of money that a landlord is willing to provide to the tenant to cover all or a portion of the build-out costs of a tenant's space.

- **Lease Term** - The more customized the build-out, the longer the term is likely to be.
  - o Office lease – Typically 3-5 year term
  - o General Retail – 3-5 year term
  - o Restaurants – 10 or more year terms
  - o Anchor tenants – 20 or more year terms

There are additional terms specific to different types of commercial properties outside the scope of this chapter that you should be familiar with if you plan to focus on commercial leasing. For example:

- **Office leasing** - often also considers issues such as building security, tenant mix, future employee growth accommodation, use restrictions
- **Retail leasing** - rent-to-sales ratio, base rent, percentage rent, breakpoints, recapture, tenant operating hours, signage and advertising, use restrictions
- **Industrial leasing** - use restrictions, inspections, specialized insurance, environmental issues

Chapter 5 - Real Estate Investing

Chapter Overview

Chapter 19 looks at what real estate investors need to know and what they might do. It starts with a look at the yield, safety, and liquidity of real estate investments. It proceeds to discuss the advantages and disadvantages of investing in real estate.

The chapter concludes with a look at different real estate investment strategies.

By the end of this chapter, you should have a basic understanding of real estate investing and can decide if this is something you want to pursue as a career. Some real estate agents start their careers focused on helping investors, and then once they accumulate some money, they start investing themselves.

Chapter Outline

About the yield of Real Estate Investments

About the Safety of Real Estate Investments

About Investing in Real Estate

You can invest in stocks, bonds, CDs, commodities, etc. You can also invest in residential and/or commercial real estate. Many financial advisors would tell you it is best to diversify. Many investors invest in commercial and/or real estate as part of your diversified investment portfolio. Other investors focus strictly on commercial and/or residential real estate.

Different types of investments generate different types of returns. The return on real estate investment takes the form of rents, additional income (for example, building advertisement), as well as an appreciation of the value of the asset (see Figure 8).

84

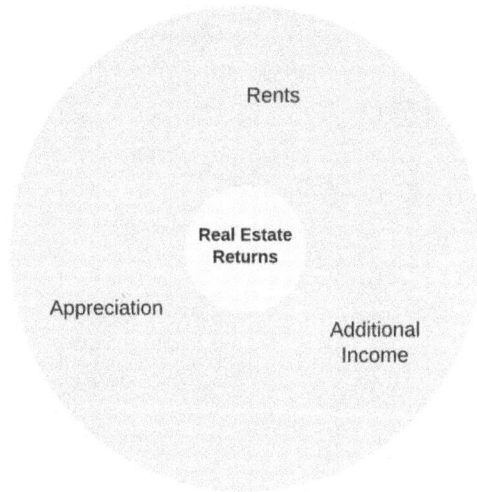

Figure 8 - Types of Real Estate Returns

Investors in real estate look at three key characteristics: Yield, Safety, and Liquidity (see Figure 9). These characteristics are discussed briefly next.

Yield

Key
Investment
Characteristics

Liquidity

Safety

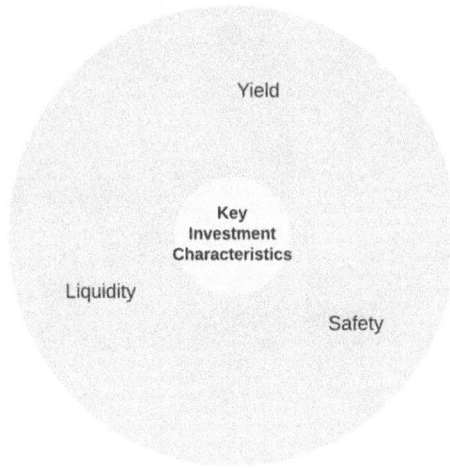

Figure 9 - Key Investment Characteristics

About the Yield of Real Estate Investments

Yield is the rate of return on the investment. Yield related rules include:

- A risky real estate investment with a low yield is not of interest to many investors.
- The riskier the real estate investment, the higher the yield needs to be to attract the investors.
- Given the same risk, an investor is likely to pick the real estate investment with a higher yield.

- Investors expect higher yields on longer-term investments as compensation for having their capital tied up for more extended periods.

About the Safety of Real Estate Investments

A safer investment is one where an investor has a lower risk of losing their money. Some investors prefer safer investments, even if the yield is lower. Others prefer higher yield and will accept the risk that goes with it.

Real Estate assets are considered one of the safest types of investments.

About the Liquidity of Real Estate Investments

A liquid investment is one that can be converted to cash quickly. Real estate assets are one of the least liquid types of assets. Typically it can take 30-60 days to sell an asset. If the asset is unique, it may take a much longer time to sell an asset, and if money is needed fast, the property might need to be sold below market value.

Advantages of Investing in Real Estate

There are four primary advantages to investing in real estate (see Figure 10):

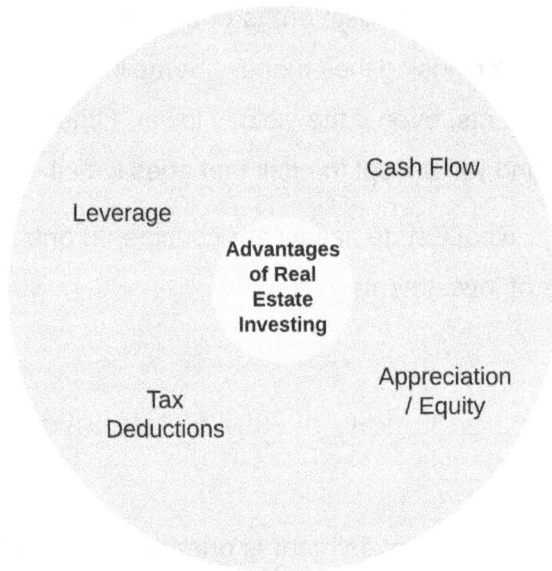

Cash Flow

Leverage

Advantages of Real Estate Investing

Tax Deductions

Appreciation / Equity

Figure 10 - Advantages of Investing in Real Estate

- **Cash flow** – the typical outcome from owning a property and leasing it to tenants for monthly income.

- **Appreciation and equity** – real estate in much of the US has shown an increase in value over time. As a property's value increases, so should your equity unless you refinance to cash out.
- **Tax Deductions** – depreciation, mortgage interest, and some operating expenses can be used as tax deductions.
- **Leverage** – using borrowed money (mortgage) to make money.

Disadvantages of Investing in Real Estate

There are five disadvantages to investing in real estate (see Figure 11):

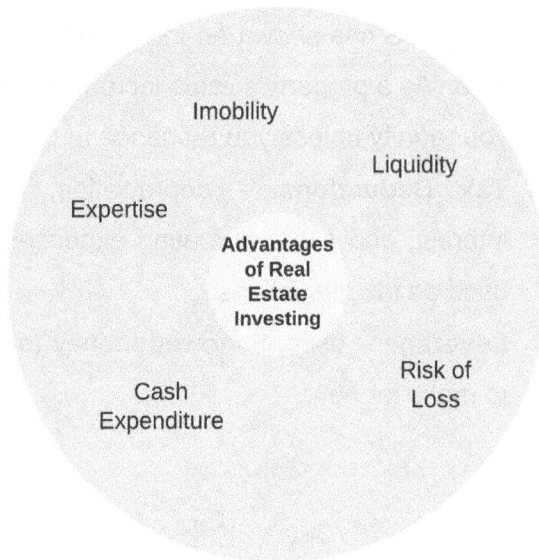

Figure 11 - Disadvantages of Investing in Real Estate

- **Liquidity** – Real estate is not a very liquid asset, as discussed earlier.
- **Risk of Loss** – in the event of a downturn when tenant(s) stop paying rent or real estate values fall substantially.
- **Cash Expenditure** – investing in real estate may require a significant amount of money as a down payment (in some parts of the country).
- **Expertise** – need to have the right agent that can identify the best deal possible for a given situation.

- **Immobility** – If a neighborhood starts to decline, your client's investment can not be physically moved. It is crucial to utilize an agent who knows how to determine long term prospects of various neighborhoods through analysis to identify where you may wish to invest on behalf of your client. "Local experts" are often biased and tell you that their neighborhoods are good to invest in.

Real Estate Investment Strategies

Properties in high priced and appreciating markets do well using the short term buy and hold strategy, where properties for lease are owned for a short period, and during that time, value is added. Some of the ways value can be added are renovating and increasing rents, and decreasing expenses.

Another short-term strategy is to fix and flip a home. You can identify fixer opportunities and experienced and reputable vendors to have the property renovated. Permits should be obtained for all work that requires permits.

You can then sell the property at a profit. Not every "fixer" property is a good candidate for this strategy. This requires a cost/benefit analysis to determine if and what level of profits to expect from a renovation.

Another investment strategy consists of purchasing a fixer, adding value, and leasing it. Some investors use this first property as leverage to purchase their next property, and so on. For example, in Los Angeles County, there are over 400 investors that own between 10 and 50 single-family homes.

Some investors start by purchasing a turnkey vacant rental property, lease it, and generate income while waiting for its value to appreciate. Other investors identify commercial properties with high vacancy rates. They replace the property management company, upgrade the building(s) and other structure(s) if necessary, increase rents, sell it, or keep it in their portfolios.

Some investors keep their portfolios for years and eventually sell them. Others pass their portfolios to their children.

Chapter 6 - 1031 Exchange

Chapter Overview

Chapter 16 looks at what 1031 exchange specialists do. It outlines the reasons to participate in a 1031 exchange. It then discusses what can be exchanged.

The chapter concludes with a discussion about each of the four types of exchanges and explains various 1031 exchange rules.

By the end of this chapter, you should have a basic understanding of 1031 exchanges and can decide if this is something you want to pursue as a career.

Chapter Outline

Reasons to Do a 1031 Exchange

What Can be Exchanged

Types of Real Estate Exchanges

Simultaneous 1031 Exchange

Reverse 1031 Exchange

Construction or Improvement 1031 Exchange

1031 Exchange Rules

About 1031 Exchanges

A 1031 Exchange is a powerful tax-deferment strategy used by real estate investors, which you might be able to turn into a career.

The term 1031 Exchange is defined under section 1031 of the IRS Code. This strategy allows an investor to defer paying capital gains taxes on an investment property when it is sold, as long as another like-kind property is purchased with the first property's sale proceeds.

Basic definitions:

- **Exchanger** - investor pursuing 1031 exchange strategy
- **Relinquished Property** – property sold via a 1031 exchange
- **Replacement Property** – property acquired via a 1031 exchange

Reasons to Participate in a 1031 Exchange

The following are key reasons for property owners to pursue a 1031 exchange:

- Defer payment of capital gains taxes

- Shift real estate investments from one type of real estate to another
- Diversify investment portfolios

What Can be Exchanged

1031 exchanges can be applied to different situations. Key among them are:

- Commercial real estate (office, retail, shopping centers, industrial, etc.)
- Residential units used to produce income (under very specific rules)
- Rental units that are part of primary residences
- Vacation homes (under very specific rules)

Types of Real Estate Exchanges

There are four types of 1031 Exchanges:

- SImultaneous exchange
- Delayed exchange
- Reverse exchange
- Construction exchange

A summary of each of these types of exchanges is presented next.

Simultaneous 1031 Exchange

A simultaneous exchange occurs when the replacement property and relinquished property close on the same day.

The exchange must occur simultaneously; any delay can result in the exchange's disqualification and make the seller pay the capital gains taxes on the sale.

There are three ways that a simultaneous exchange can occur:

- A swap or a two-party trade, where the parties exchange (swap) deeds with one another.
- A three-party exchange where an "accommodating party" is used to facilitate the transaction.
- Simultaneous exchange with a Qualified Intermediary (QI) who structures the exchange.

Delayed 1031 Exchange

A delayed exchange is the most common type of exchange, allowing up to a maximum of 180 days to purchase a replacement property. A qualified intermediary must be engaged to complete a delayed exchange. The three steps of a delayed 1031 exchange are detailed next (see Figure 12).

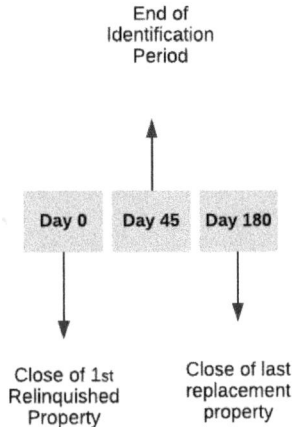

End of
Identification
Period

| Day 0 | Day 45 | Day 180 |

Close of 1st
Relinquished
Property

Close of last
replacement
property

Figure 12 - Delayed Exchange Timeline

Sale of the Relinquished Property

Before closing the sale of the relinquished property, the exchanger must enter into an exchange agreement with a qualified intermediary. Based on the exchange agreement, an assignment is executed before closing, and the qualified intermediary assumes the exchanger's Purchase and Sale agreement. The QI instructs the escrow officer to deed the property from the exchanger to the buyer directly. Proceeds are transferred directly to the QI, thus protecting the exchanger from receipt of funds.

Identification of Replacement Property

The exchanger must identify potential replacement properties within 45 calendar days. The identification must be made in writing, and the property must be clearly described. The three rules of identification are:

- **Three Property Rule**: An exchanger can identify a maximum of three (3) replacement properties without regard to the properties' fair market value.
- **Two-Hundred Percent Rule**: The exchanger can identify any number of properties as long as the combined fair market value does not exceed two-hundred percent (200%) of the fair market value of the relinquished property.

- **Ninety-Five Percent Exception**: The exchanger can identify any number of properties with the combined fair market value exceeding 200%, as long as the properties acquired amount to at least ninety-five percent (95%) of the fair market value of all these identified properties.

Purchase of Replacement Property

The exchanger has 180 calendar days from the closing of the relinquished property to acquire like-kind replacement properties. Before closing on the replacement property, the exchanger assigns the Purchase and Sale Agreement to the qualified intermediary. The qualified intermediary then purchases the replacement property with the exchange funds and transfers it back to the exchanger by a direct deed from the seller.

Reverse 1031 Exchange

A reverse 1031 exchange, also known as a forward exchange, occurs when the exchanger acquires a replacement property through a QI before exchanging the property they currently own.

The exchanger has 45 days to identify what property is going to be sold as the relinquished property.

After the initial 45 days, the exchanger has 135 days to complete the sale of the identified property and complete the reverse 1031 exchange with the replacement property's purchase.

Construction or Improvement 1031 Exchange

The construction exchange allows the exchanger to make improvements on the replacement property by using the exchange equity. The exchanger can use their tax-deferred dollars to enhance the replacement property while it is in the hands of a qualified intermediary during the 180 days.

This type of exchange has three rules:

- The entire exchange equity must be spent on completed improvements and/or a down payment during the 180 days.
- The exchanger must receive "substantially the same property" that they identified by day 45.
- The replacement property must be equal or greater in value when it is deeded back to the exchanger. The improvements must be in place

before the exchanger can take the title back from the QI.

1031 Exchange Rules

There are several rules to follow when exchanging properties. These rules are presented next (See Figure 13).

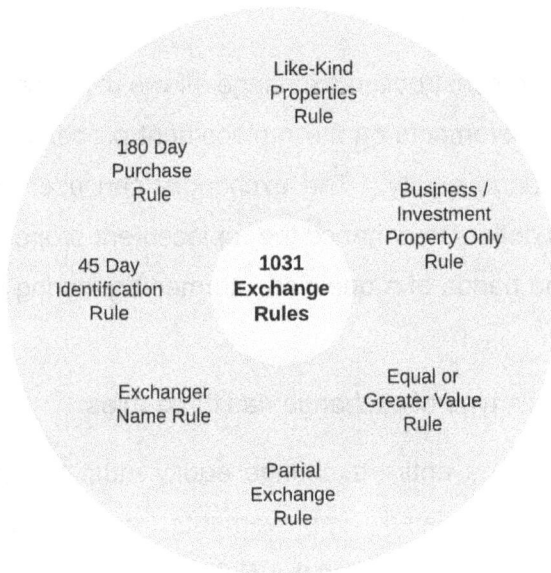

Like-Kind
Properties
Rule

180 Day
Purchase
Rule

Business /
Investment
Property Only
Rule

45 Day
Identification
Rule

**1031
Exchange
Rules**

Exchanger
Name Rule

Equal or
Greater Value
Rule

Partial
Exchange
Rule

Figure 13 - 1031 Exchange Rules

Exchanging Like-Kind Properties Rule

To qualify as a 1031 exchange, the relinquished property and the replacement property must be like-kind. Like-Kind property means that both the original and replacement properties must be of "the same nature or character, even if they differ in grade or quality".

1031 Exchanges can include more than two properties. For example, the exchanger can exchange one property for multiple replacement properties or exchange multiple properties for one property.

- Any type of real property, except for a person's primary residence, can qualify for a tax-deferred exchange. However, the rules for exchanges require that the relinquished property and the replacement property are "like-kind" to one another.

- "Like-kind" does not mean that the relinquished property and the replacement property must share the same physical characteristics. For example, a shopping center does not need to be exchanged for another shopping center. It can be exchanged for an industrial warehouse, an apartment building, etc.

- "Like-kind" refers to the requirement that property be "held for investment or for productive use in a trade or business" must be exchanged for other property that is also "held for investment or for productive use in a trade or business."

Business or Investment Property Only Rule

A 1031 exchange is only applicable for business or investment property. It does not apply to personal property. Also, you can not exchange one primary residence for another.

Equal or Greater Value Rule

To defer paying 100% of the taxes for the sale of a property, the IRS requires the net market value and equity of the replacement property to be the same as or greater than the relinquished property.

Partial 1031 Exchange Rule

The exchanger can carry out a partial 1031 exchange, in which the replacement property is of lesser value, but this will not be 100% tax-free. The difference is the amount the exchanger will have to pay capital gains taxes on. This option makes sense when a seller wants to get some cash-out and is willing to pay some taxes to do so.

Exchanger Name Rule

The name appearing on the relinquished property title must be the same as the name on the tax return and the same as that of the titleholder buying the replacement property. However, a single-member LLC can sell the relinquished property, and that sole member may purchase the replacement property in their name.

45 Day Identification Window Rule

The exchanger has 45 calendar days, after closing of the relinquished property, to identify (in writing and provide documentation to the QI) one or more replacement properties, based on the three rules (3 Properties rule, 200% rule, and the 95% rule) discussed earlier in this chapter.

180 Day Purchase Window

It is necessary that the replacement property is received and the exchange completed no later than 180 days after the sale of the relinquished property or the due date of the income tax return (with extensions) for the tax year in which the relinquished property was sold, whichever is earlier.

Chapter 7 - Real Estate Auction

Chapter Overview

Chapter 15 presents the benefits of auction and the differences between auction sales and standard real estate sales. The chapter then proceeds to look at different types of auctions. Next, the chapter details the various steps of the auction process.

The chapter concludes with a look at some specific scenarios common to auctions of real estate assets.

By the end of this chapter, you should have a basic understanding of real estate auctions and can decide if this is something you want to pursue as a career.

Chapter Outline

Benefits of Real Estate Auction

Differences Between Ordinary Sales and Auction Sales

Auctions with Reserve

Auctions Subject to Seller Confirmation

Absolute Auction / Auction without Reserve

Important Terms of the Auction Contract

Bidder Registration

Terms Included in Auction Advertising

Due Diligence Prior to Auction

Switch to Auction if Can Not Sell via Ordinary Sale?

Auction Sale for Occupied Property with No Interior Access?

About Real Estate Auctions

Auctioning real estate properties is not something most agents handle, but depending on your personality and communication skills may be of interest. Auctions are very popular in some parts of the US and relatively rare in others.

Going once, going twice…. Sold! These statements are what make auctions fun and exciting. An auction is generally a public sale of property to the highest bidder conducted by an auctioneer. The auctioneer's goal is to obtain the best financial return for the seller by free and fair competition among bidders.

Some define real estate auction as the public sale of real estate, in which the sale price offered is increased by competitive bids until the highest accepted bidder becomes the purchaser. Competitive bidding is a fundamental part of real estate auctions. It's the competition that pushes the price up, higher and higher.

Benefits of Real Estate Auction

There are multiple important benefits to conducting a real estate auction (see Figure 14). These include:

- The seller knows when the property will sell

- The seller sets a reserve price and does not need to be involved in the negotiations process
- Buyers arrive ready to purchase the property
- Includes a comprehensive marketing program that maximizes interest and visibility
- Exposes the property to a large number of pre-approved prospective buyers
- Requires potential buyers to pre-qualify for financing
- Accelerates the sale
- Reduces ongoing carrying costs, including taxes and maintenance, due to quick disposal
- Creates excitement leading to increased competition among buyers, which can result in auction price exceeding the price of a negotiated sale
- Ensures that property will be sold at true market value

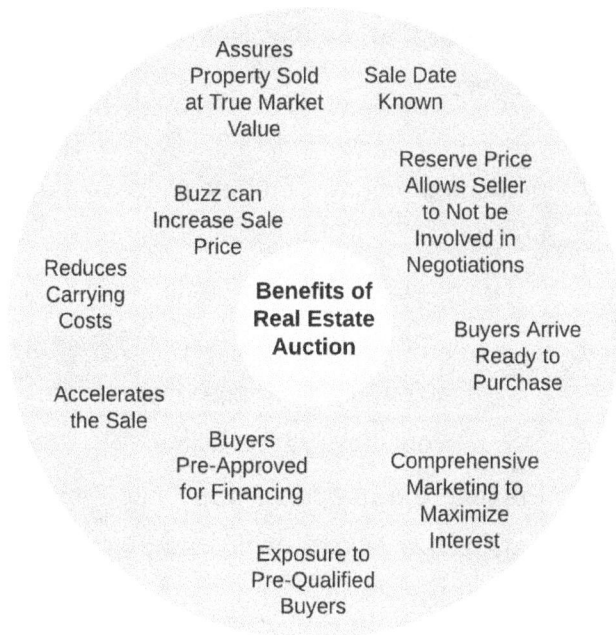

Assures Property Sold at True Market Value

Sale Date Known

Buzz can Increase Sale Price

Reserve Price Allows Seller to Not be Involved in Negotiations

Reduces Carrying Costs

Benefits of Real Estate Auction

Buyers Arrive Ready to Purchase

Accelerates the Sale

Buyers Pre-Approved for Financing

Comprehensive Marketing to Maximize Interest

Exposure to Pre-Qualified Buyers

Figure 14 - Benefits of Real Estate Auction

Differences Between Ordinary Sales and Auction Sales

In an Ordinary Sale:

- The seller does not know exactly when the property will sell.

- The seller can set a reserve price in their mind but needs to be involved in the negotiation process.
- The sale can include a comprehensive marketing program that maximizes interest and visibility
  - However, most agents simply place the property on the MLS, and from there, it automatically propagates to other websites such as Zillow.
- Present the property to a large number of prospective buyers, which may or may not be qualified.
- It can require potential buyers to be vetted, providing financing pre-approval and proof of funds; however, many agents do not do that.
- Some buyers that submit offers are ready to purchase, while others are not.
- The sale can be accelerated if the property is listed at the bottom of the comps or below the comps.
- Quick disposal is possible if the property is priced at the bottom or below the comps, thus reducing long term carrying costs.
  - However, most agents do not list at the bottom or below the comps.

- Some buzz and excitement leading to increased competition among buyers can be created.
  - Price property very competitively.
  - Set a quick deadline to submit offers.
  - As soon as the second offer comes in, inform everyone there is a multiple offer situation.
  - As soon as the first offer above the asking price comes in, start informing everyone you have offers above ask.
  - As soon as the first cash offer comes in, start informing everyone your offers include all-cash offers.

As you can see, it is possible to simulate excitement and competition similar to that created in an auction by conducting ordinary sales using the right strategies. However, for various reasons, most agents are not able to accomplish this.

Auctions with Reserve

An "auction with reserve" is an auction where the seller establishes a reserve on a property and is subject to the seller's confirmation – sellers are not obligated to confirm a sale other than at a price that's acceptable to them. The reserve is the minimum price that a seller is willing to accept for the property to be sold at auction. In an auction with a reserve, the property offered will sell to the highest bidder only if the auctioneer accepts the highest bid and declares the property sold.

The auctioneer is not required to disclose the reserve price at the auction and generally doesn't do so. The seller reserves the right to accept or reject the highest bid within a specified time. Once a bid is submitted that exceeds the reserve price, the property can be sold to the highest bidder. The auctioneer can announce that the reserve has been met, and the property will sell today in an effort to generate more bids. This type of auction reduces the seller's risk since the sales price must be above a minimum acceptable level.

Potential buyers may not invest the time and money in due diligence in reserve auctions since there is no certainty they will be able to buy the property even if they are the highest bidder. This type of auction limits interest to those buyers willing to pay the minimum bid price, and so has to be low enough to attract bidders.

For example, your seller wants to sell real property and believes its value is $1,000,000. If they do not want to risk selling the property for less than it is worth, you can place a reserve on it. The auctioneer should assist the seller in establishing the reserve. In this instance, the auctioneer may establish a reserve price of $950,000. The reserve will prevent that property from being sold for an amount less than $950,000. You can reject the bids or withdraw the property if bids come in lower than $950,000.

Auctions Subject to Seller Confirmation

At an auction that is subject to the seller's confirmation, the seller does not establish a minimum bid or reserve. Instead, they simply reserve the right to reject any and all bids regardless of price or justification. The auctioneer will present them with the highest bid made for the property after the bidding. They will then decide whether to accept the bid and sell the property or not.

There is no certainty as to the selling price. The seller can accept the highest bid or reject it. Until the highest bid is received, the seller does not need to make any specific determination. This type of sale can be used for any kind of property but may be particularly helpful when it is difficult to determine the property's value. This would reduce the risk of setting the reserve either too high or too low.

Absolute Auction / Auction without Reserve

In an absolute auction or an auction held without reserve, the property is sold to the highest bidder, regardless of the price. This type of sale generates the maximum response from the market, and buyer excitement and participation are heightened.

Mutual contingent assent is achieved when an offer is made. Each bid made is a mutual assent between the seller and the respective bidder, contingent only on no higher bid being received. As each high bid is made, the previous contract is extinguished, and a new contract based on mutual contingent assent comes into being. When no further bids are made, the last bid's contingency is extinguished, and a final contract in the series of contingent contracts is established.

Therefore, absolute auctions are not marketed as subject to seller confirmation, lender approval, financing, minimum bid, or anything else. An absolute auction is a sale to the highest bidder with no limiting conditions.

This has its risks. Some believe real property should be sold subject to any liens at a reserve auction. The owner and the auctioneer should discuss setting the reserve price at an amount that will allow the owner to pay the balance owed for any lien and/or mortgage. An auction with a reserve will assure the owner that they will not be responsible for paying the difference between the selling price and the amount owed on the mortgage or lien. It is discouraged to approve the sale of property with a mortgage, or any type of lien on it, at an auction without reserve.

Important Terms of the Auction Contract

The key terms of an auction contract include:

- Exclusive right to sell the property
- Address of the property to be sold
- Term/duration of the contract
- Place, time, and date of the auction
- Auctioneer's duties and obligations
- Whether the sale is with or without reserve
- If there is a specific reserve, the reserve amount
- Authority of the auctioneer to act on behalf of the seller
- Authority of the auctioneer to charge a buyer's premium
- Acceptable methods of payment
- Seller's duties and obligations
- Liability for damage to property

- Sellers's representations and warranties (Clear title, ability, and authority to sell)
- Description of the property to be used at the auction
- Seller's acknowledgment of risk in the sales
- Liens and encumbrances
- Compensation of auctioneer (commission)
- Payment of expenses (e.g., advertisement costs)
- Arbitration clauses or alternative dispute resolution terms
- Other miscellaneous provisions

Bidder Registration

Bidders are required to register for the auction before the sale. The registration process clarifies the terms of the sale contract. When bidders register, they typically show their driver's license or another form of identity, provide contract information, and execute a document containing the sale's essential terms. By executing the registration agreement, the bidder accepts the terms and conditions of the sale and agrees to be bound by them. The terms and conditions outlined in the registration form should supplement and complement any terms announced by the auctioneer before the sale. After registering for the sale, the bidder is provided with a bid card and bid number.

Terms Included in Auction Advertising

Specific terms should be included in an auction advertisement. These items include: (1) the time, place, and date of the auction; (2) general description of the property or lots to be sold; (3) any disclaimer of warranties; (4) notice that a buyer's premium will be charged, if any, and the percentage amount; (5) any deposit requirements; and (6) in a minimum bid auction, the minimum price should be stated.

Included should be information that could help prevent a dispute. For example, an advertisement could notify the public that the seller has the right to withdraw the property from the sale or cancel the sale. This will help protect the seller and reduce the likelihood of complaints or litigation due to the withdrawal of property or the sale's cancellation.

In addition, the advertisement could give notice that the property is being sold as-is. The ad's information would help prevent others from arguing that they did not know the property was being sold without any warranties or in an "as is" condition.

Due Diligence Prior to Auction

To avoid liability, auctioneers must know what they are selling. As part of the due diligence for a real estate sale, the title search verifies that the seller owns the property and identifies any liens. The liens that may be found during a title search include, for example, mortgages, mechanic's liens, judgment liens, and tax liens. These items will usually need to be resolved before the closing.

In some instances, auctioneers ask for a property survey to provide additional clarity of what is being sold. A survey of the parcel will reveal any encroachments on the property and verify the acreage. Encroachments can include easements, disputed property lines, fence issues, and improperly installed driveways.

Switch to Auction if Can Not Sell via Ordinary Sale?

If you are unable to sell a property via ordinary sale, you could consider an auction. You can also make a massive price reduction that will, at the right price, bring lots of offers, including offers over ask if you underprice the market.

Alternatively, you can perform a series of quick smaller price reductions (weekly, for example) until offers start coming in.

If you need the money asap, preparing for and properly marketing an upcoming auction may take 30 days. Once in escrow with a cash buyer, a minimum of a couple of weeks may be requested. The same can be accomplished via an ordinary sale where the property is placed on the MLS if the list price is substantially below the market to quickly attract a large audience.

Auction Sale for Occupied Property with No Interior Access?

Before jumping to sell with no interior access, ask, why is there no interior access? You might get immediate interior access if you provide the tenant with a 24 hour Notice to Enter. Interior access for showings and inspections will provide a greater return on the sale of the property. You can also attempt to negotiate Cash for Keys with the occupant if rent is not being paid and get the property vacant.

If you have any ideas for improvement of this book please email me at david@GeffenRealEstate.com or text me at 310-433-0694

If you enjoyed this book, please consider posting a review. Even if it's only a few sentences, it would be a huge help. Thank you.